YPS

YESHIVA PIRCHEI SHOSHANIM
ישיבה פרחי שושנים

Pirchei Publishing
146 Village Path / P.O. Box 708
Lakewood, New Jersey 08701
(732) 370-3344
www.shulchanaruch.com

Edited & Compiled by YPS:
Rabbi Shaul Danyiel & Reb Ari Montanari
www.lionsden.info/YPS

BUSINESS ETHICS

COURSE CONTENT

PIRCHEI SHOSHANIM SHULCHAN ARUCH PROJECT

Business Ethics

Leadership

Lesson One

62 African Street, The Gardens, Johannesburg, South Africa tel. 082 745 8731

Table of Contents:

Leadership

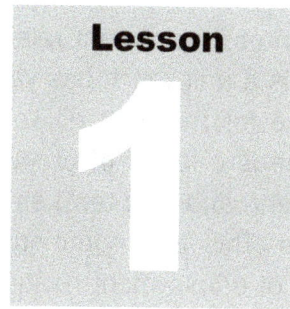

Introduction and Lesson Objectives

In this module, we will explore the characteristics of ethical leadership. Ethical leadership is a study of how leaders and leadership activities can be a powerful influence on ethical and moral behaviour. We will explore some contemporary leadership models – with particular relevance to transformative leadership and the creation of ethical organisations and leadership styles and character traits. We will then cast our focus on classical Torah leaders whose vision transformed their followers and shaped our own history. Lastly, using these models and examples, we will consolidate the principles of ethical leadership and the obligations on those in a position to influence others.

All discussions revolving around business ethics are by necessity issues of leadership. Most texts dealing with leadership and the ethical organisation start by discussing concepts such as the triple-bottom line and the environmentally sustainable business. The core values espoused by an organisation and issues such as fair-play, corporate philanthropy and productive work environments all originate within the leadership of an organisation. This lesson will focus on effective leadership and illustrate how this is a precursor to effective ethical decisions.

Contemporary Leadership Models – Transactional Versus Transformational

We all know instinctively that much of our behaviour is goal driven. We work harder towards the achievement of those goals we value. It would seem natural therefore that all organisations and leaders would identify what their employees' value the most and use it as an incentive to drive greater productivity. Research indicates, however, that in most cases, management fail to make the connection between goal-driven behaviour and a productive workforce [1].

This introduces the idea of the *transactional leader* - one who assists his followers in the achievement of their goals. By understanding what it is people want, how to administer what they want and point out the connection between great performance and reward, a leader facilitates *transaction* – an exchange of mutually rewarding behaviour.

This form of employment relationship is defined as the *transactional* model. Each piece of work is a unit which has value to the organisation. The organisation remunerates the employee for that unit of work at a market related value. In this sort of climate, the employee is a factor of production, his output is measured according to the return on investment, and long term employment is based purely on current or future utility to the business. This is a common trend in organisations today and characterises a large number of employment relationships. This is by no means a terrible scenario; the basic needs of the organisation and the employee are met. The limitation is that the transactional leader fulfils short-term needs. He achieves the immediate needs of the organisation by fulfilling the immediate needs of the employee. Neither he nor his followers is committed to the other - they will continue to transact as long as the exchange is mutually beneficial.

This limitation is overcome through *transformational leadership*. If we consider human needs holistically, an individual requires significantly more than remuneration. If we consider that a massive proportion of one's life is spent in economic activity or at work, the linear approach of transactional leadership will never fulfil diverse human needs or take advantage of diverse human competencies.

Transformational leaders strive to share a vision with their followers and grow their followers by challenging, guiding and inspiring. The rewards for achieving the goals of the group become internal and intrinsic. Transformative leaders don't just position goals and motivators to be attractive to the employee; they challenge the philosophy and culture of a group [1]. We can all agree that many of the greatest leaders in history were revolutionaries and visionaries.

Bass [2] identifies the three factors belonging to the transformational leader:
1. Charisma – He instils value, respect and pride in his followers. His ability to articulate a vision depends on this.
2. Individual attention – He pays attention to his followers' needs and assigns meaningful projects and tasks. He does not overlook small people or small issues.
3. Intellectual stimulation – He encourages creativity in others and ensures that everyone around him is using their abilities to the maximum.

Researchers have identified a specific skill set unique to transformational leaders. The required skill-set includes assessment skills, communication abilities, sensitivity to others, the ability to identify skills and skill deficiencies in others and the ability to articulate a vision. While many of these skills are often innate to exceptional leaders, these abilities can also be shaped and honed through experience, challenge and education.

Classical Leadership & Examples in Our History

In classical Jewish thought, Moses embodies all the traits of a quintessential Jewish Leader. Several episodes in his development as a leader and subsequent appointment as leader of a nation, illustrate some of the critical moral dilemmas and opportunities that create exceptional leadership. We can certainly distil some leadership lessons we can employ in our lives and businesses. We will also contrast his leadership style with that of Elijah the Prophet and uncover some important differences between crisis-time leadership and long-term principles in successful leadership.

A major theme which permeates the lives of our greatest leaders is their concern for small things and attention to detail. Small acts demonstrate the greatness of an individual. An effective analogy is that of the Silo. While it is impossible to determine the complete contents of a silo, we need to see what comes out of it. If a small hole at the base of the silo allows small quantities of grain to escape, we can conclude that the entire structure is filled with grain. Small, easily overlooked acts of kindness demonstrate a greater repository of kindness. Even small actions represent the contents which cannot be seen.

Early Signs of Potential

The first indication that Moses is destined for leadership occurs in Exodus 2:11 "*and Moses grew and went out to his Brethren and saw their suffering*" [3]. Surely the act of going out is a sufficient precursor to seeing suffering? By being present at an event do we not automatically experience an event? Why is the act of seeing distinguished from the act of going out? **Rashi** [4] explains that he was not simply struck by the pain they were experiencing. Anybody would have been able to identify the pain they were experiencing. There is nothing particularly special about noticing things which are immediately evident. Rather, Moses deliberately geared himself so that he would be able to fully experience and understand the full extent of their suffering. He went beyond the realm of his senses and tried to empathically experience the pain. Only that complete experience would allow him to understand and connect fully to their needs. From this we can understand the first principle of Moses' leadership:

1. Great leaders take pains to notice what their followers are experiencing. They should always be connected in some way and be fully cognisant of the pain and challenges of their charges and employees. No person or issue will ever be taken for granted.

The Burden of Leadership

At times the burden of leadership can be overwhelming. It is tempting for any leader to withdraw from the responsibilities of his position and point the blame at the intransigence of his followers. At one point, when his charges have become fractious and rebellious, Moses cried to G-d *"... Did I give birth to [this nation] that you have instructed me to carry them..."* [5]. What is the nature of this instruction Moses alludes to? What instruction from G-d does Moses feel is beyond him? **Rashi** on this verse quotes the **Sifri**[6] who explains as follows: G-d commanded Moses to lead with the clear understanding that the people he is leading will not follow easily. They may come to rebel, question his authority, insult him and even resort to violence. Moses is required to fulfil a position which will often put him in direct opposition to the people he cares for. He is required to deal with the myriad demands of these people, many of which fly directly in the face of his Divine instructions. The reality of leadership is that difficult choices must sometimes be made which never gain popular support.

2. A true leader will be required to say and do things which may be unpopular with his followers. He may even be required to challenge his peers and question the status quo. His leadership may need to weather this opposition. This may be even more painful because his decisions are for the benefit of others.

Continuity and Character – Choosing a Replacement

As Moses' tenure ends and his death approaches, he prays *"G-d of the spirits, appoint a man...let the assembly not be like sheep that have no shepherd...Take Joshua... a man in whom there is spirit"* [7]. Moses is displaying another rare leadership trait. A great litmus test of good leadership is the concern he shows after his tenure has ended. If he continues to show caring even after it is no longer his concern, we can safely conclude that his original concern was legitimate. Moses' concern for the well-being of his followers does not stop as soon as his appointment ends. His first concern is that a suitable succession will take place.

3. Responsible leaders ensure that others are in place to safe-guard their legacy, renew the vision of the organisation and care for the well-being of its constituents. Continuity plans are put in place long before they should be necessary.

However, perhaps more important than the idea of continuity, are the qualifications hinted to in the verse. What is the significance of the word *spirit* which is repeated above *"G-d of spirits....man...in whom there is spirit."* **Rashi** explains the verse: *G-d of the Spirits*: The personality of every individual is revealed before You – no two people are alike. Only You can decide the appropriate appointee who is able to deal with each person according to their personality. *Joshua...spirit:* God replies that Joshua would be the best replacement since he is able to act in a manner befitting the personality of each individual. He will be able to understand the minutiae of every personality and know exactly what challenges and assistance every individual needs to grow to their full potential.

4. A basic trait in a leader is sensitivity to individual differences. To maximise the contribution of each individual, we must see how they can contribute to the group as well as how to develop those abilities. By setting appropriate tasks and providing appropriate guidance, every individual can flourish under his care.

Elijah – Fight or Nurture? Two Personality Types

Elijah is undoubtedly one of the most enigmatic leaders in Biblical history. He confronts hundreds of false prophets and brings down a massive conflagration. He approaches falsehood undaunted and single-handedly leads a campaign against the status-quo. He undoubtedly represents dominant, authoritative leadership. One episode however draws his values in sharp contrast with those of Moses. After his confrontation with the prophets of idolatry, he finds solitude and describes to an angel the zealotry he had shown in the name of truth. G-d responds by showing him terrible acts of nature: a hurricane, followed by an earthquake followed by fire – followed finally by a still, small sound. The **Malbim** explains: The great acts of nature were destructive and powerful, but only achieved destruction. The thin small sound represents overpowering patience: the ability to talk to others, and convince and influence them. By showing impatience and taking the route of extreme authority with others, Elijah lacks a critical leadership trait. While his extreme actions may have been necessary under extreme circumstances, he could never guide these people without a large amount of patience and willingness to guide them. This contrasts strongly with Moses who repeatedly asks for mercy and grace for those under his guidance. Elijah is thereafter instructed to find a new spiritual leader – one who has the necessary patience to guide the People of Israel. His actions are appropriate for the crisis he encountered but are unsuited for the demands of ordinary leadership.

5. Although the ability to make demands, choose battles and enforce discipline may sometimes be needed; effective leadership is also characterised by patience and a genuine desire to grow and develop those in one's care.

A Central Tenet: Don't Misguide / *Lifnei Iver*

When identifying the primary ethical role of the leader in a business setting, there is one Torah injunction which broadly covers the actions of any leader. The Torah states: "You shall not curse the deaf nor place a stumbling block before the blind..."[8] The **Minchas Chinuch** [9] explains that a purely literal reading of this verse doesn't serve much purpose since the Torah already protects people against any physical harm. It is rather a requirement that we do not in any way mislead or take advantage of others who are unsuspecting and ignorant of our true motives. In this respect, they are morally blind, relying on others to assist and guide them in all areas of life.

This verse is often analysed with respect to business transactions and is dealt with as such over the remainder of this course. Here, however, it takes on a particular relevance. The **Midrash Sifra** [10] explains that whenever we provide advice but fail to account for our own self-interest fully, we place a stumbling block in front of the blind. Often our motives in providing advice go unquestioned by ourselves or the recipients of our advice. As our next session will illustrate, self-interest is sometimes particularly difficult to identify. As leaders, we have vested interest in our opinions and ideas for many reasons. The leader must always ensure that his guidance of others does not feed his self interest to the detriment of his followers.

Questions for Review

1. What characteristics of transformational leadership are displayed by Moses?

2. What business advantages can be gained through the application of transformational leadership?

3. What are the practical limitations in our culture of transactional work-practices?

4. Should our hiring processes reflect the idea of leadership skills or are core competencies more desirable?

5. In career counselling, what possible conflict of interest scenario could 'place a stumbling block' before a junior employee?

6. How is leadership markedly different from traditional management?

Sources

[1] Bernard.M.Bass, "From Transactional to Transformational Leadership: Learning to Share the Vision," Organisational Dynamics, Winter 1990, pp. 19-31

[2] Bernard.M.Bass, Leadership Perfromance Beyond Expectations (New York: Academic Press, 1985)

[3] Shmos 2:11 "vayar besivlosam"

[4] Rabbi Shlomo Yitchaki: 1040 – 1105

[5] Bamidbor 11:12 "heanochi harisi..."

[6] Sifri 91

[7] Bamidbor 27: 16 – 18

[8] Vayikra 19:14

[9] M.C 232:4

[10] Vayikra 19:14

PIRCHEI SHOSHANIM SHULCHAN ARUCH PROJECT

Business Ethics

Alternative Dispute Resolution

Lesson Two

62 African Street, The Gardens, Johannesburg, South Africa tel. 076 187 1451

Table of Contents:

Alternative Dispute Resolution

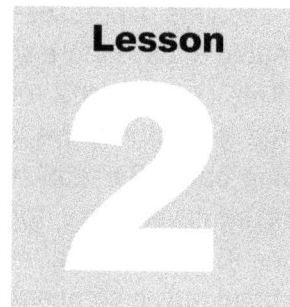

Lesson 2

Introduction and Lesson objective

In times where litigation is expensive, slow and contentious, alternative forms of dispute resolution become increasingly attractive. Most law firms offer professional services in mediation and different forms of arbitration and the alternative dispute resolution (ADR) arsenal has become fully stocked with creative, flexible solutions. The core philosophy behind ADR is rooted in the belief that conflict, while a natural outgrowth of human and business interactions, does not have to result exclusively in Win-Lose or Lose-Lose scenarios. While ADR has become a viable legal route globally, we may neglect that the rabbinic tradition has a strong tradition of dispute resolution and a well established system of legal procedure. From the perspective of our secular court system, the Beis Din is itself a form of alternative dispute resolution. This session aims to introduce you to the ideas, processes and philosophy underpinning the Torah system of litigation and dispute resolution.

The purpose of Halacha (Jewish Law)

The **Chazon Ish** [1] gives us an incredible tool to understanding the link between ethical behaviour and Jewish Law. He explains that ethical obligations are often intrinsically linked to *Halacha*. Moral imperatives should not be divorced from the body of the law; rather the Jewish law should be used as guideline in understanding the boundaries of ethical responsibilities. To illustrate this point, the Chazon Ish describes the following scenario: In a small town with established Torah teachers, a new group of teachers arrives from an adjacent town. As is the nature of people, the residents were not fully satisfied with the old and immediately jumped to enrol their children with the new teachers. As a result of this, the established teaching body suffered financial loss. The established teachers immediately sought to undo the damage from the newcomers. These new-comers who had damaged their livelihoods became the subject of a counter-campaign. The established teachers pointed out their deficiencies and limitations and sought to gain support from the townsfolk. All their actions were a response to the thoughtless encroachment of the new-comers and their actions were justified in light of their victimhood. In fact, their actions against the new-comers can be treated as ethically beneficial. Since they are fighting against interlopers with no sensitivity for the livelihood of others, these actions are highly commendable. That is however, until we learn the

Halacha. The **Talmud** states that '*Kinas Sofrim Tarbeh Chochmah*' – The competition between scholars increases wisdom. With that understanding, we learn that it is commendable to have more scholars in town – because through that, we have increased wisdom. This reverses the role of the new-comers and their opponents. When viewed through the lens of intuitive logic, we feel able to establish the wronged party and the wrong-doing party. Our ethical conclusion is based on our ability to distinguish wrong from right intuitively. The Torah however first creates a point of reference for us. It establishes in *Halacha* the '*rodef*' (the pursuer) and the *nirdaf* (the pursued). With this halachic boundary, a compass point has been set. From that reference point, the gamut of Jewish moral behaviour can be established comparatively. In our scenario, the established teachers have sought to damage the new-comers without an acceptable pretext. Their behaviour becomes ethically questionable. The Torah is ordinarily extremely concerned with fairness in economic competition, this scenario however offers marvellous insights into the nature of endeavour and the high value placed on wisdom.

Beis din: compromise, arbitration & Din Torah

Often, as parties approach the *Beis Din* (Jewish Court), they will meet with an adjunct to the *Beis Din* – called a *Safra Dedayna* (Literally: Scribe of the Beis Din) who fulfils secretarial, administrative and procedural duties. The *Safra Dedayna* may assess the merits of the case and try to advise the parties regarding their options to resolve the dispute. Prospective litigants who approach the *Beis Din* are always strongly encouraged to first mediate and arbitrate their dispute before formal litigation takes place in the Beis Din.

Mediation or *pshorah* encompasses the notion of voluntary compromise. As in contemporary mediation, the Rabbi mediating the case will suggest but not enforce various compromise scenarios. There is a clear social benefit to this form of compromise. Ultimately, the mediator can focus on the communal benefits of reaching a compromise. The effects of more serious intervention will likely result in irreconcilable differences. An early compromise will ensure that a potential fall-out does not carry broader, more damaging social consequences. An agreement will result in each party making a *kinyan sudor*.

In Arbitration or *bitzua*, the parties accept the potential outcome before the case is heard. A single Rabbi will usually arbitrate the case and the outcome of the finding is binding. In this case, the parties will make a *kinyan sudor* even before an outcome is reached.

A traditional *Din Torah* or formal court appearance involves three *Dayanim* (Judges) who deliberate on the case put before them. A person required to attend *Beis Din* as a party to the dispute or to provide support, receives a *Hazmonah* (subpoena). While the exact process in Beis Din has no exact structure and may differ slightly from one Beis Din to another, the process is one of seriousness and deliberation. The *Dayanim* try reach 'pshorah koruv le'din' – a suitable resolution which most resembles the strict law but may synthesise additional legal and circumstantial requirements. The ruling of the *Beis Din* is binding on the parties. The *Beis Din* has several sanctions at its disposal. If a defendant fails to appear at the request of the Beis Din, the *Dayanim* may issue a *shtar siruv* which may permit the plaintiff to pursue the case in a secular court.

What involvement may Lawyers have in a *Beis Din*?

Understanding the legal status of an attorney in *Beis Din* is invaluable to understanding the rights of the parties but also helps illustrate some ideas behind the functioning of *Beis Din*.

The **Shulchan Aruch** [2] states that a lawyer may not represent a defendant since the defendant himself is more likely to speak truthfully. However, the concept of *shlichus* (appointing a substitute) has bearing in Jewish law. Why should another person not be allowed to stand in his stead and make his case for him? The **Chazon Ish** [3] explains that in this case, the principle of truth is even more compelling than the principle of representation, and therefore a lawyer cannot talk in the place of the defendant. This does not fully negate the principle of representation, as we will see.

May the plaintiff (claimant) have a lawyer represent him? The sages of the Talmud instituted a form of representation call *Harsha'ah* (literally: permission) which allows another person to make the claim on their behalf. The purpose of this representation is to allow a representative to follow the defendant in the event that he leaves the city and file suit in a distant location. This will allow the plaintiff to continue his dealings without the significant loss of chasing after the defendant. The **Shach** [4] explains that this will even extend to allowing his representative to accompany him even when he is present. The implication of this allowance is that the plaintiff may be allowed an attorney but the defendant may not.

The **Aruch Hashulchan** [5] states that it was the prevailing custom in his community to allow attorneys to represent each party. Indeed, the prevailing custom in many *Batei-Dinim* (plural of *Beis Din*) today is to allow lawyers to assist each party.

The **Chazon Ish** [6] helps to align the principles of Talmudic law with the prevailing custom today. We can distinguish between an advocate and a substitute. In the case of *Harsha'ah* above, the substitute acts with all the power and rights of the plaintiff. An advocate however, is appointed to provide counsel and to represent the argument of his client clearly and effectively. Ultimately, the Chazon Ish requires that each party provide explicit consent to the presence of legal counsel in the *Beis Din*. If any party objects to the presence of his adversaries counsel, his request should be respected.

With this in mind, we can look back at the original concern of the Talmudic sages. If truth is of greater import than the assistance of a lawyer, then we should keep in mind the following: The **Talmud** [7] quoted by the **Shach** [8] states that a litigant and his representative must be extremely careful to represent their case in a truthful manner even if they believe that fraudulent testimony will assist them in correcting an injustice. The ultimate purpose of the attorney in *Beis Din* is to ensure that the testimony given is as accurate as possible, not to try and provide an unfair advantage.

Appealing Judgement – Getting a Second Opinion From Another Rav?

In traditional litigation, court systems ordinarily make allowance for appeals based on the idea that the law is sometimes open to various opinions and understandings or even misunderstandings. It appears logical that any system which is dedicated to uncovering truth and creating an objective illustration of reality will therefore be extra cautious to allow for multiple viewpoints and an opportunity for appeal to a higher authority.

The Torah tradition however, intentionally, does not make much allowance for appeals or consulting other authorities in everyday issues of Jewish law. There are however, compelling reasons for this trend, many of which are based on the Jewish concept of law. The **Talmud** [9] relates a fascinating story regarding the wife of Rav Nachman. She related a question regarding family purity to Rabba Bar Rav Chana. She was however, dissatisfied with his response and appealed his ruling to Rav Yitchak who reversed the original ruling. The Talmud is justifiably troubled by this event. It relates the principle that one Rabbi may not reverse the decision of a colleague. The Talmud resolves this scenario by concluding that the scenario was unusual in that Rabba Bar Rav Chana was in this particular case not able to determine the situation correctly – something the second Rabbi was able to do.

Some early commentators provide reasons behind the limitations on reversing earlier rulings. The **Ran** [10] explains that the concept of 'Torah' itself is undermined in that "Two Torahs" are created. This is an unusual statement. Surely the reality is, only one Torah exists and the other opinion must be wrong? Surely every time we find a conflicting opinion among the Sages of the Talmud or among contemporary Rabbis, "Two Torahs" are also created? This can partly be answered by the answer of the **Raavad** (quoted by the Ran) who states that every time someone presents an issue for deliberation to a Rabbi, he imposes a form of vow upon himself (*shavya anafshei chaticha deissura*).

The **Baalei Tosafos** [11] present two alternative resolutions to the Talmudic episode above. They explain that the second Rabbi may indeed reverse an earlier ruling provided that the questioner discloses the fact that he had already received a strict ruling previously. It also requires that the second Rabbi can produce convincingly clear proof that the original ruling was erroneous (*Taus BeShikul HaDa'as*). The Tosafos also understand that a second Rabbi might indeed investigate more thoroughly and uncover an error in the original judgement.

The **Rema** [12] ultimately rules that an original judgement can always be overturned, provided the original judgement was blatantly incorrect. 'Blatantly incorrect' in this case refers to a *'dvar mishna'* – a universally accepted halachic practice. He may not overturn a judgement relating to a subtle interpretive difference upon which there may be no clear consensus (*shikul hada'as*). Even then, the Rema requires that the original Rabbi retract his ruling in the face of the clear evidence.

The **Aruch Hashulchan** [13] concludes that if the second Rabbi is more senior, he is authorised to counteract the ruling of the first. He bases this opinion on the fact that seniority is based on reasoning ability and the fact that his argument is likely to be more convincing. However, if the original Rabbi is the leader of a community or shul (*Mora De'asra*), then his rulings should not be overturned. It is critical that appropriate respect should be shown for such a figure and the authority of the spiritual well-being of the community not threatened.

Appealing *Beis Din* – can mistakes happen?

While we have established that appellate divisions are common in western law; what allowance do we make in the Jewish legal structure for appeals?

The **Talmud** [14] relates scenarios in which a *Beis Din* may reverse its own decisions with particular relevance to cases in which obvious mistakes are made; as opposed to issues of subtlety and deliberation. The **Talmud** [15] does however state that one *Beis Din* cannot challenge the ruling of another *Beis Din* (*Beis Din Basar Beis Din Lo Dayki*). The **Shach** [16] understands this to mean that no *Beis Din* can rehear a case which has already been judged by another court.

In Israel today we see the phenomenon of a Supreme Rabbinical Court of Appeals. How can such an institution exist today based on the above ideas. Indeed, a Jewish court of appeals is a relatively new concept. **Rav Ovadia Yosef** [17] argues for the inclusion of such an entity. He argues that it is entirely permissible to allow an appeal court to review the decisions of the previous *Beis Din*. The injunction is against rehearing the case from the beginning. If their primary purpose is to ensure that the decision making process of the previous court was correct, then it serves only to protect against error. He adds that the lower courts issue their ruling as binding only in a case that the appeals court does not reverse it. This also fits according to the Aruch Hashulchan who understands that a Rabbi of greater stature should be allowed to reverse a ruling.

While it appears that reversal of decision is permissible under certain conditions, Jewish tradition makes no formal allowance for the concept of appeals. The reality in most of the world, with the exception of Israel, is that most communities will determine the necessity of such measures themselves and implement them where necessary.

Advice to the Arbitrator: The Philosophy of Investigation and Truth

Rabbi Dessler [18] points out that the very nature of investigation is linked to one's curiosity or interest in an idea or issue. Furthermore, we are often invested in finding a particular outcome before our investigation even begins. The experimental hypothesis often requires that the researcher first take a position and propose a probable hypothesis. The researcher would have no point of reference from which to investigate, if he did not first have a clear interest and investment in the answer. This is the starting basis of most day-to-day problem solving. Our beliefs, biases and experiences provide the framework from which we draw probable solutions.

The process of judging the truth in a case however demands greater exactitude and cognitive awareness. A person, who wants to understand the ethical boundaries of tax avoidance, is usually trying to avoid paying more tax. A salesman who wants to know what features of his product he has to disclose usually has one or two he would rather not publicise. The starting point of most investigation usually involves definite interest in the investigating party. How then is someone who is resolving a dispute or is required to discover the truth able to remove his natural bias from the situation? Can an arbitrator or judge ever be fully neutral?

The **Talmud** [19] brings the following challenge. Can a judge take a gift from one party to a dispute, without showing favour to that party? If he is offered an 'incentive'- not to favour one party - rather to encourage him to review the facts of the case as thoroughly as possible. Surely if a person accepts the gift but still endeavours to judge accordingly, he can separate himself from the self-interest the gift might create. The Talmud resolves that once he has 'connected' to one party in this fashion, he no longer has the inherent ability to view them objectively. He is naturally drawn to the opinion of the giving party and is less likely to make a judgement which contrasts with his new (albeit sub-conscious) worldview. His natural problem solving ability is coloured by his new experience.

The Torah presents the following law. "Listen between your brothers, and judge them righteously". The **Talmud** [20] explains: This is a warning to the judgement panel that they shouldn't hear the case of one party to a dispute before the other party has arrived and a warning to the parties that they should not make their case before the other party has arrived. The **Maharal** [21] elaborates: Even if there is no question of dishonesty or intention to mislead, the judge will form an opinion based on the testimony of one party and will likely develop a positive perception of the first party's position. Even though the judge has no intention of maintaining that position and is aware that the second party is likely to have just as compelling a story, he has – for one moment - favoured one side. Once a person has a pre-conception, we have to work even harder to change his mind. A person experiences a discomfort when their preconceptions are challenged (Cognitive dissonance). The tiny amount of commitment he has placed in the first testimony means that upon hearing the second testimony, he carries the hair-breadth of a prejudice. According to our tradition, that is already sufficient means to affect the outcome of judgement.

Rabbi Dessler suggests that in our ordinary dealings, real objectivity is extremely unlikely. However, in situations where we are required to distil the truth from circumstances, we must be motivated by an innate desire to uncover the truth, uncover our own motivations and clarify our thought processes.

Questions for review

1. How does Beis Din offer a viable form of ADR (alternative dispute resolution)?

2. How does Halacha (Jewish Law) benefit the formation of ethical behaviour?

3. What is primary directive of Beis Din - Justice or Peace?

4. What benefits and disadvantages do Lawyers offer the Beis Din process?

5. What is the general Jewish approach to 2nd opinions from Rabbis?

6. What is the role of the arbitrator or judge and how does it affect his conduct?

Sources

[1] Emunah and Bitachon 3:1
[2] Choshen Mishpat 124
[3] Choshen Mishpat 4
[4] Choshen Mishpat 124
[5] Choshen Mishpat 124
[6] Choshen Mishpat 4
[7] Shavuos 31a
[8] Choshen Mishpat 75
[9] Niddah 20b
[10] Avodah Zorah 1b Bedapei Harif
[11] Niddah 20b; Avoda Zora 7a
[12] Yorei Deah 242:31
[13] Yoreh Deah 242:62
[14] Sanhedrin 33a
[15] Bava Basra 138b
[16] Choshen Mishpat 19:3
[17] Teshuvot Yabia Omer 2: Choshen Mishpat 2
[18] Michtav MaEliyahu pg 52
[19] Kesuvos 105b
[20] Sanhedrin 7b
[21] Nesivos Olam, Nesiv Hadin

PIRCHEI SHOSHANIM SHULCHAN ARUCH PROJECT

Business Ethics

Corporate Philanthropy

Lesson Three

62 African Street, The Gardens, Johannesburg, South Africa tel. 076 187 1451

Table of Contents:

Corporate Philanthropy

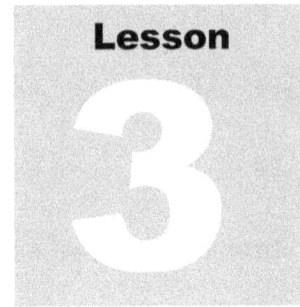

Introduction and Lesson Objective

Corporate Philanthropy is a growing trend in developed western countries. In the Unites States, corporate philanthropy is a big business, with most large organisations funding a philanthropic arm which re-channels charitable funds in the arts, venture philanthropy and community outreach. The idea of corporate philanthropy, however, does not always find an easy home in big business. The Ford Foundation, one of the largest philanthropic arms in the United States today, has had no association with its parent – the Ford motor company for over 30 years. It was discovered that the aims of philanthropic foundations did not always find alignment with the goals of capitalism. Some foundations, such as the Lauder foundation, whose roots lie with its Jewish founder, donate millions of dollars to Jewish causes around the world and are actively involved in outreach projects.

This session aims to qualify the concept of corporate philanthropy in Jewish ideals and practice. Should our companies even be vehicles for charity or patronage? Milton Friedman argued passionately that the only moral obligation of the enterprise is to make as much money as possible. Perhaps charity should be a personal act and our businesses should only be the vehicle to make profits; profits which can then be distributed in our own personal capacity. The largest bequests ever made, are still primarily from individuals divesting themselves of their fortunes, not from companies who are usually trying to make money. We will now try and understand some of the principles governing our conduct in charity and how our businesses should conduct themselves outside of the business process.

Darchei Sholom – Creating Harmony

Mr. Edelman runs a large plastics plant near a township and employs a large number of people from the surrounding area. He is always involved with local charities and tries in his own capacity to take care of his employees, show compassion and ensure that their basic needs are taken care of. After starting a small crèche for his employees, he is approached by an aid organisation to assist in setting up a larger feeding scheme - under the banner of his business - across the broader indigent community. They explain to him that his contributions will help feed communities in many cities and provide excellent exposure for his business. They assure him that his contributions will be tax effective since they have set up the appropriate tax deductable structures. He is however, slightly ambivalent. He wishes to contribute to their scheme, but he is aware that the *Chevra Kadisha* also asked him to increase his contributions drastically to assist in the economic downturn. He is unsure if he can meet both commitments.

The **Talmud** [1] introduces the idea of *darchei sholom* – ways that foster peace. The agricultural resources which are usually made available to all the poor of the town are also open to the use of poor from other communities – regardless of whether they are Jews or Gentiles. The **Ran** [2] clarifies the wording in the Talmud. He states that one might think that the obligation to look after all the poor of a city – including Jews and non-Jews will only apply when the poor of your own community come to collect the agricultural resources left for them. One might think that since your own poor are eating, we should not cast off those that join them in taking advantage of the grain. He explains that the wording of the Talmud requires us to allow all the needy of the city access even when the poor of our own communities do not wish to take advantage of this boon. This is one of the actions which fosters additional harmony. The Talmud places a priority on *darchei sholom* – even alongside the ordinary priorities of charity. Ordinarily we ensure that the poor of our own town are taken care of first – we certainly have no obligation to deal with others until all of our own local poor are satisfied first. We can see from this that generating peace among people and being part of a functional society still carries value. This does not however change the fact that the most destitute and closest to us take priority.

The **Shulchan Aruch** [3] states that we should see no contradiction in feeding the poor of other communities, visiting the sick, burying the dead and comforting mourners even though they belong to another religion or cultural group. He explains that all these activities, positive deeds which we most commonly perform amongst members of our own communities, are indeed desirable since they foster harmony and peace between neighbours. Additionally, the **Shach** [4] sees no contradiction in providing resources for the poor of another community that you don't specifically provide to your own.

There is however a requirement that the poor of your own town and community are taken care of first. Once we have discharged the basics of that obligation, we should take the needs of others into account. We will discuss some of the ways in which we are required to give of our resources.

Tithing – G-d as a Business Partner

Mr. Kopelowitz has a large amount of shares in a public company. He receives significant dividends from his ownership and attends all the shareholder meetings. He has tried to introduce the idea of corporate philanthropy to the CEO and board but they have not taken his requests seriously. They contend that while his idea is admirable, their only obligation is towards the profits of the shareholders. Mr. Kopelowitz wishes to ensure that the money he has received also has a chance of contributing to others and he has decided to affix a percentage of his profits for local charities and schools. Even though the business itself will not contribute, he wants to ensure that his own business dealings carry greater import.

There is a generally accepted practice in Torah circles to pay *ma'aser* (tithe) on our income. The source of this activity varies between scholars. The status of this activity is viewed by some as a tenet of the Torah and by others as a *minhag* (customary practice). The **Talmud** [5] quotes the verse in the Torah [6] "you shall surely tithe" (*'Asser Ta'Asser'*). Even though there is some contention as to whether this verse refers to the monetary tithing we perform today or not, Rabbi Yochanan states that the words of the verse can also be read as "tithe so that you can become wealthy". He explains that a person can use this verse to test G-d. If he gives his *ma'aser* unfailingly, he can expect to receive the promised reward of wealth. The **Baalei Tosafos** [7] state that the tithing referred to in the Talmud incorporates agricultural activity as well as all business income, salaries or even gifts. **The Vilna Gaon** [8] even expresses a more extreme requirement. He states that one is required to give up to a fifth of one's income to charity as long as legitimately deserving people and charities still approach him. He can only be said to have discharged his obligation to give once he has given 20%. His ruling would only apply in the case of one who has already provided for everything he possibly requires for his own family. Most commentaries however do not require someone to make such a significant contribution and indeed, most people give 10% customarily. We can however see from his ruling the significance of charitable giving in our tradition.

Mr. Kopelowitz should ideally consult a list of local community charities as well as establish - with a resident Halachic authority - the ideal amount and distribution of his money.

Priorities in Giving

Let us take a closer look at Mr. Edelman's conflict. He is aware that he should make an effort to ensure that the poor of his own community are dealt with first, but he is concerned that that the feeding scheme may be significantly more urgent. How do we prioritise the concept of need as well as community?

It has also become a global trend that companies and individuals give charitably to crises around the world. It has become almost fashionable to make online pledges and donations every time a catastrophe occurs. The idea of charity and volunteerism is a global movement and more people want to get involved. This is undoubtedly one of the most positive trends of this decade. We are still required to ensure that our contributions achieve the best possible impact and that the causes we contribute to are legitimate. Where should we start?

The verse states "When there will be a needy person from among your brethren, in one of your gates in your land that the Lord your G-d has given you, don't harden your heart and don't close your hand from your needy brother. Surely open your hand and lend him according to his need that is lacking to him" [9]. **Rashi** on this verse explains that the word used for 'needy' is different from the word usually used to describe poverty. From this he concludes that need is a variable when deciding where to give first. The word 'shearecha' – 'your gates' indicates that the poor of your city should be considered first.

We should therefore balance our contributions between local organisations and recipients; then we should consider recipients in other places but still linked to us. We should still then contribute to causes of deprivation outside our communities that have the greatest need.

The Corporation and the Environment

Corporate philanthropy often involves far more than community outreach; many organisations have become avid protectors of the environment and are placing their precious philanthropy funds into areas of environmental sustainability, conservation, green business models, preservation of species and animal anti-cruelty. These are all factors of social and ethical concern and many can be linked to Torah principles.

The verse states "When you besiege a city for a long time, while making war against it, to take it, do not destroy its trees by swinging an axe against them."[10] The term used for this destruction is *tashchis*. The **Talmud** [11] adds to this requirement that the unnecessary destruction or wastage of any item or resource is forbidden. The Talmud introduces the concept of *baal tashchis,* the broad injunction against wastage and destruction. The ramifications would be that any unnecessary destruction is a Torah injunction and can be treated as a priority in environmental initiatives.

The **Talmud** [12] instructs us regarding the appropriate treatment of animals. The Talmud illustrates a scenario whereby an animal becomes trapped on the Sabbath. The Sages discuss the permissibility of extricating the animal in a way which is acceptable on the Sabbath. The Sages agree that it is appropriate for one to provide as much alleviation of distress to the animal as is permissible until such a time as the animal can be fully rescued. Animals which we own must be treated humanely according to Divine law and therefore certain Rabbinic enactments may sometimes even be set aside if it leads to conflict with this concept. This goes as far as permitting certain Rabbinic enactments on the Sabbath to be put aside to ensure the well-being of these animals.

There are indeed a large number of sources which show sensitivity for environmental issues, the wellbeing of animals, the protection of the environment and species. We should therefore balance the need to participate in the maintenance and preservation of the environment with more demanding human issues. Ultimately, we place a higher value on the protection and welfare of humans when choosing where to place our resources. However, the endless list of human problems and concerns should in no way discharge our environmental obligation. We should ensure that our businesses are environmentally aware and certainly in cases where there is little risk or interference with charitable giving to other people, we should certainly ensure that we uphold these principles.

Accepting money from the Government or Corporations

There is a little known ruling in the **Shulchan Aruch** [13] regarding obtaining funding for communal needs from sources outside of the community. The Shulchan Aruch states that one should not take charity from the government publicly and in cases when the internal resources of the community cannot sustain it, then the money should be taken without much external show. In a case where the money is given as a gift, we should certainly not return it, but we may distribute it to the indigent in outside communities without publicising its source. We learn from this ruling the idea of self-sufficiency. When seeking funding from corporate or government sources, we should take this idea into account and try balancing the needs of the local community, the philanthropic actions of the enterprise involved and the need to maintain self-sufficiency. These decisions may be very hard to calculate without the input of an expert in these issues.

We should not be dependant on sources of income that may ultimately be to our detriment. We must be consistently aware of the sources of the money we obtain and the ramifications of the actions of those that donate to our causes. The decision regarding where we obtain our money can sometimes be just as important as the source of our money and the way we make our money.

Questions for Review

1. Are patrons of the arts justified in investing their money in cultural institutions such as galleries and concert halls before they contribute to social needs?

2. Should corporations be involved in philanthropic giving? Does it detract from their core function or is it a redeeming activity?

3. What forms of environmental involvement are likely to be closest to the Torah concept of environmentalism?

4. Should schools and yeshivas be considered as important as charities and food distribution networks?

Sources

[1] *Gittin 59b*

[2] Gittin 27b Bedapei Harif
[3] Yoreh Deah 152:12
[4] Yoreh Deah 152:12
[5] Taanis 9a
[6] Devarim 14:22
[7] Taanis 9a
[8] Sefer Shaarei Rachamim 45
[9]Deuteronomy 15:7-8
[10] Shmos 20:10
[11] Shabbos 129a
[12] Shabbos 128b
[13] Yoreh Deah 254

THE PIRCHEI SHOSHANIM SHULCHAN ARUCH PROJECT

Business Ethics

2010 business Opportunities – Trademarks, Counterfeiting and Merchandising

Lesson Four

Table of Contents

2010 Business Opportunities –
Trademarks, Counterfeiting
and Merchandising

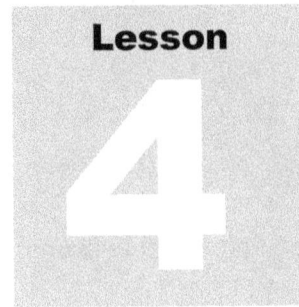

Lesson

4

Introduction and Lesson Objective

As 2010 approaches, we have been repeatedly exhorted by industry pundits and the government to take advantage of the event and ensure that South Africa takes maximum advantage of the economic benefits that the anticipated tourist influx is likely to bring. While many hospitality experts have planned ahead and are ready to host visitors from around the world, many entrepreneurs are still trying to find a viable business that can take advantage of the short-lived burst in economic activity. Central to this challenge is the use of the official event trademark and patents. The production of promotional merchandise is already subject to tender and not legitimately available to anybody for production. We may however wish to use the trademark in conjunction with an existing product in order to promote its attraction to people who are excited about upcoming events or maybe are considering manufacturing similar looking products which may be popular with people who don't want to pay a premium for 'original' products.

The question of patents, trademarks and counterfeiting goes well beyond our scenario. The software, music and film industry is trying to fight the largest copyright infringement movements ever encountered. Trademark infringement is par for the course in the largest manufacturing economy in the world and the open-source and creative-commons movements have changed the game rules regarding ownership and intellectual property. We will attempt to elucidate some of the fundamental rules and ethics regarding intellectual property and try distil the essence of what poses a contravention in *Halacha*.

Counterfeiting

Although we will establish the exact boundaries of the rulings on intellectual property, it is instructive to see how the community may treat a traditional counterfeiter.

Rabbi Feinstein [1] discusses the case of someone involved in forging money and the risk he poses to those around him. He quotes the **Rama** who rules that someone involved in the activity of forgery or counterfeiting may endanger those around him. Ultimately, when his activities are discovered, it may result in a backlash from the Government or Monarchy who may persecute the innocent due to their involvement with such an individual. Because he trades in illicit currency, his neighbours will eventually trade – unknowingly – in the counterfeit currency he has distributed and become implicated in his scheme. In this situation, the community must hand him over to the authorities to prove that his actions were isolated and that they do not support his fraud. This ruling is unusual in that ordinarily we endeavour to avoid handing other Jews over to the authorities on the basis that they may be judged excessively harshly beyond the restitution required by the Torah. In this case however, he poses a real danger to other people and instead of resolving the problem internally; he should be handed over immediately. People whose actions pose a threat to others will ordinarily be treated the same way.

The **Rama** quotes the **Maharam Ma'Riesburg** who rules even in a case where someone is hurting the livelihood of others by trading in counterfeit goods – and not just posing a threat to their freedom – we are authorised to take action against him. The community must instruct him to cease his dishonest practice. If he has been warned and he still won't cease, he can be handed over to the authorities. He adds that especially in a case where someone is being investigated unjustly, he can then point out the real culprit.

Theft of Intellectual Property

The **Talmud** [2] states that someone who digs a pit in the public domain is considered as if he owns the pit even though it is not really under his ownership. The idea is reflected in the fact that he is responsible for guarding the perimeter of the pit to ensure that it does not cause injury or damage to others. The 'owner' of the pit is liable for damages caused by it even though he has no actual share in the public area in which it is located.

Rabbi Shimon Shkop [3] uses this concept to explain the ownership of intellectual property. Just as the pit is in the public domain and thereby rendered ownerless, intellectual property becomes distributed in the public arena and is no longer under the control of the originator. This explanation helps us understand how something which is no longer under a person's control can still be considered their property. If, according to Rabbi Shkop, intellectual property falls under the concept of ownership, we can then conclude that intellectual property should fall under the rubric of all laws of ownership and thus becomes subject to the implications of theft and misuse. The idea behind Rabbi Shkop's analogy is very novel and many disagree with his conclusion. Indeed, it is argued by many that property can never be something as insubstantial as a phrase, a song or even a picture. Once a person takes a book and publishes it or posts a picture in a public archive, they effectively lose control of the resource and ownership becomes impossible. These opinions rely on other rulings to render copyright and trademark infringement a reality.

Another approach to the issue of intellectual property is based on the **Nodeh Beyehuda** [4]. He bases the issue on the concept of *'ze neheneh v'ze chosar'* – One person benefits from the loss of another person. His ruling concerns the right of an author to the type-setting he paid for. In this case, the typesetting was of a work traditionally in the public domain. If the printer maintains ownership of the type-setting, his printings will compete with the original printings of the author and cause him financial loss. His argument would follow that if someone can claim ownership of something in the public domain, then certainly an author or originator can claim ownership of an item which is ostensibly their property. The central idea is based on the understanding that by using someone else's intellectual property that we would have otherwise paid for, we cause the originator unnecessary loss. This would apply to copying a textbook that the student would have been forced to purchase and certainly applies to someone who produces counterfeit goods which cause the originator to lose revenue.

The **Chasam Sofer** [5] brings another argument in favour of the protection of intellectual rights. The Talmud rules that a fisherman must keep his fishing nets a fish-swim length away from a fish which has been targeted by another fisherman. This is a fascinating idea. The only claim the fisherman has on the fish is the fact that he has already invested some energy in trying to trap it. This is not an actual acquisition; by dint of his effort however, we treat it as his property and any attempt to catch it is considered encroaching on his livelihood. There is no concept of theft per se, since the fish is still technically ownerless. The idea of encroachment is called *Hasagas Gvul* – encroaching on the boundary [of another person's income]. The Chasam Sofer treats any use of intellectual property as encroachment. The creator has invested effort into his idea – he has laid claim to its use on the basis of his effort and any infringement on that 'ownership' undermines his claim. Using the trademark or patent will cause another's income to be unjustly reduced.

From the last two ideas, we can already identify a pattern in understanding the treatment of intellectual property. The first concept which treats intellectual property similarly to real property will carry the most stringency. If intellectual property carries similar ownership to real property, then one should not make use of it without permission. If it is used, then the owner can only claim compensation if he loses from the transaction. The second and third opinions don't treat intellectual property as real property. Rather they consider the implications of its use. According to them, one may probably be justified in using intellectual property provided one can guarantee that its use will not cause loss to the originator and not infringe on his income.

This is only a cursory examination of these ideas. Each case of usage would have to be evaluated by a Halachic expert. We can however consider a few scenarios.

Mr. Kaye wishes to print 2010 t-shirts and sell them at traffic lights. He is not placing any trademarked patterns on the shirts. We can assume that in doing so, Mr. Kaye does not infringe according to our opinions above. Since his t-shirts are not technically counterfeit, he is not copying a product which is likely to cause another loss.

Mr. Frankel is running a B&B in his house over the world cup. He wants to place a world cup emblem on his website so that over-seas visitors can see that he is looking for 2010 patronage. Although the emblem is a trademark, unless he actively misleads potential clients that he is accredited by a 2010 body, he might be permitted to put it on his website. He certainly causes no actual financial harm to the trademark owner if he had no intention of purchasing its rights in the first place. There may however be other factors such as *dinah demalchusa* and *gneivas daas* which might prevent him from using the trademark.

Mr. Goldman is producing authentic-looking world-cup soccer balls which he intends to sell outside stadiums. He has copied the official soccer ball design and is mass-producing the product in China. This scenario may pose more complications than the other. In addition to using the World Cup design, he is undercutting Mr. Salzman who has purchased the rights to sell real world cup paraphernalia outside the stadiums. Every soccer ball which Mr. Goldman sells may eat into the margins and livelihood of Mr. Salzman. According to the Maharam Ma'Riesburgs ruling, the counterfeit activity is treated very seriously in its encroachment on another's income.

Other Applications

There are many different applications for the concept of intellectual property, many of which we don't even consider. If intellectual property is something we need to be cognisant of, are we permitted to wear clothing which has been 'copied off' a designer label? Should we be allowed to use unique recipes which are supposedly trade secrets? Are we permitted to listen to music which another person has downloaded from the internet? How should we treat internet based peer-to-peer networks which allow people to openly share software, music and other copyrighted material? These are exhaustive topics, some of which create contention in the understanding of ownership. This session is not intended to resolve every issue of intellectual property but rather to start establishing the ethical boundaries which surround ideas like copyright and counterfeit.

Questions for Review

1. Can an employer make claim to the intellectual creations of an employee which he creates during non-productive time in the office?

2. Rabbi X. is being investigated for tax fraud after his accountant used the shul accounts to run a tax-evasion scheme. Is he permitted to point out the culprit?

3. If one manufacturer's counterfeit 2010 clothing is of a poor quality, should he also be sued for damage of reputation?

4. How is the encroachment (not theft) an issue in intellectual property rights?

5. What basis might a person have to make use of another's intellectual property without permission?

6. Should someone be permitted to take the World Cup trademark designs and 'Photoshop' them so that they portray an amusing message which one can sell on t-shirts?

Sources

[1] *Choshen Mishpat 388*
[2] *Bava Kamma 29b*
[3] *Chiddushim Bava Kamma 1*
[4] *Nodeh B'Yehuda Choshen Mishpat 24*
[5] *Choshen Mishpat 41*
[6] *Orach Chayim 40:19*

THE PIRCHEI SHOSHANIM SHULCHAN ARUCH PROJECT

Business Ethics

Dinah D'Malchusa - The Law of the Land

Lesson Five

62 African Street, The Gardens, Johannesburg, South Africa tel. 076 187 1451

Table of Contents:

Dinah D'Malchusa – the Law of the Land

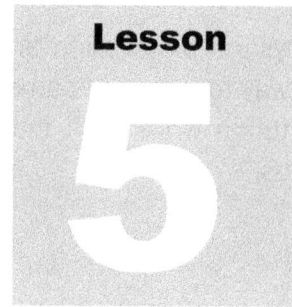

Introduction and Lesson Objectives

In the session we discuss the concept of *Dinah Demalchusah Dinah* – 'The law of the country in which you live is applicable to you'. It appears to be a sensible edict regarding people who live in a country as a distinct group – slightly separated from those around them. We can reason that, as Jews, who are traditionally singled out for differences in behaviour, we should be additionally careful in our conduct among the nations. While we explore the reasoning behind this edict in this session, we can anticipate that complications will arise when we try meld Torah law with state law. They are by no means the same – and while some of the ethical imperatives which underlie each system may overlap – they are ultimately different. In order to develop a system in which Torah law and state law co-exist, we need to understand the purpose of *Dinah Demalchusah Dinah*, and establish the boundaries and purpose of Torah law.

Introduction to *Moser*

Central to this purpose are several key ideas and definitions. Firstly we must distinguish between the concept of Jewish Courts and Secular courts. To do this, we should explore the concept of the *Moser* – the Jewish informant. The **Rambam** [1] teaches that one Jew may not hand over another to the secular authorities; not his money or his body. This is a potentially contentious law. Superficially, one might understand this rule to be an attempt to circumvent the natural course of law and protect people who are deserving of punishment. This is by no means the purpose of the prohibition. If one subscribes to the Torah ethical code, we accept that the system of Torah sanctions and infringements is carefully weighed. Our concern is not that people should be subject to an 'outside' system; rather that people may suffer unnecessarily and be punished beyond that which the Torah system prescribes. It is therefore not an opportunity to lie to authorities or close ranks. Not only are there restrictions on what must be dealt with 'internally', but for the idea of *Dinah Demalchusah* to apply, we obviously must draw the line at some point. Secular courts are a greatly desirable force. The Sages of the Talmud teach us that the establishment of courts of justice is one of the *mitzvos* (commandments) which is mandated upon all mankind. Secular courts and legal codes are critical for the functioning of any society. This being so, our intention in using our own courts where possible is not intended to undermine the authority of the state - rather to strengthen the

Torah system of sanction and remedy. The Torah deals with most issues of theft in a similar way to issues of damages. In traditional legal systems, damages may be an issue of restitution while theft may incur significant jail terms. We will now explore several scenarios.

Is it Permissible to Hand Over a Thief to Secular Courts?

The bookkeeper for an established business, over several years, manages to fraudulently skim funds from several accounts. By the time forensic auditors locate the theft; many hundreds of thousands of rands have been successfully spirited away. The directors of the company, once informed of the problem by the auditors, are unsure of the correct response. Being that everyone in the company is Jewish, they are aware that there is a concept that Jews should ideally be judged in a Jewish court but are unclear about the exact circumstances and procedure to follow. They want to initiate an action which will allow them to get their money back as well as ensure that the bookkeeper does not get away with the act. Surely calling the police straight away might be best?

Rabbi Moshe Feinstein [2] outlines the issue as follows: If the directors hand the thief over to the state, it is highly possible that the bookkeeper will be punished by traditional legal standards. There is however the concern that the perpetrator is likely to suffer for his crimes significantly beyond the remedies that are set out by the Torah. In all business interactions between Jews, the Torah outlines sanctions which allow the guilty party to make full reparation for his deeds. Each sanction is exactly weighed against the severity of the crime so that the punishment fully rehabilitates the negative consequences of the action. In Torah law, theft is primarily resolved through restitution, not jail terms. Rabbi Feinstein adds that there are some actions that western courts would not consider illegal but that Jewish law censures strongly. In such a case also, a secular court system would fail to take into account the Jewish ethical implications of the action and the perpetrator would never remedy the transgression. We can see from here some of the rationale behind the idea of avoiding secular courts if applicable. We are not attempting to resolve the issue extra-judicially; rather we want to ensure that the corrective action taken corresponds exactly to the nature of the damage caused.

The **Talmud** [3] relates a case about the punishment fitting the crime. Reish Lakish was assigned to guard an orchard from theft. An intruder entered the orchard and ate figs from the trees without payment. Reish Lakish shouted and attempted to drive him off. The intruder ignored him and continued his theft undaunted. Reish Lakish cried out to him that he would henceforth be excommunicated (*cherem*). The thief replied: If I owe you money, that is one matter, however I have not yet done any act which warrants the severity of excommunication. Reish Lakish went to the *beis medrash* (house of Torah study) and enquired whether his *cherem* was valid. The scholars informed him that his excommunication was not applicable to the crime; a situation Reish Lakish was then forced to reverse. This case illustrates that monetary issues can only attract the penalties ordinarily associated with them.

The **Talmud** [4] however also relates a scenario regarding Rabbi Elozor ben Shimon. He advised a policeman regarding an effective system for identifying and catching thieves. His system worked so well, the government hired him to investigate and catch thieves himself. He would locate people who were sleeping at certain times of the day and proceed to prove that they were involved in larceny during the night and hand them over to the authorities. This vignette would seem to contradict the injunction against the *Moser*. Rabbi Feinstein contends that in such a case, Rabbi Elozor may indeed be permitted to hand these men over to the authorities. Since he is employed to perform these duties, there are certain exceptions governing his conduct. What difference should his employment make to his obligations? Surely even taking such a position is a problem in itself? The case of Elozor ben Shimon is relatively extreme and it appears from the Talmud that the Sages did not fully approve of his actions. Our next scenario will help explain the constraints placed on someone who is employed by the government.

Beis Din may find that it is necessary to refer the theft of the bookkeeper to a secular court. The primary issue here is that the *Beis Din* should be the first point of reference in ascertaining the correct course of action.

When a Jew is the Tax Man

Mr. Goldberg is approached by SARS to work as a tax inspector. After many years as a forensic auditor and tax expert, they want him to join as a senior team member and help boost their tax collection efforts. Mr. Goldberg is however, concerned about some of the implications of his job. While he is a supporter and proponent of full compliance, he knows that many of the companies he will audit are Jewish owned. If he uncovers any tax irregularities, he will obviously need to report their indiscretions just as he would any other business. He doesn't want to create any conflict of interest with Torah ideals by taking the job. Is it better to avoid the position altogether?

Rabbi Moshe Feinstein [5] explains that someone in the above position will most likely have to be required to report other Jews to state authorities. The concern is not that they should not be held accountable for their actions, but rather that the state may prosecute them at a stricter standard than the Torah requires. Rabbi Feinstein explains that there is in fact no real conflict in a Jew taking such a position. The very nature of the position is such that anyone with the appropriate qualifications can fill it. If he doesn't take the job, someone else will. Regardless of who takes the position, any tax evasion committed by a Jewish firm has an equal chance of being uncovered by any auditor. The implication is that in such a position, he cannot inflict any more harm on the transgressors than they would ordinarily be open to anyway. Since the entire injunction is based purely on the potential harm he inflicts on the person he hands over, here there is no problem in the performance of his job. If his presence would mean that people would suffer greatly as a result of his intervention, then he would certainly be held liable.

This view is supported by the **Talmud** [6]. The Talmud discusses the case of one who leads the agents of the King to confiscate the assets of another person. The King is exercising his power to attach the belongings of any person in the realm and the scout is forced to use his knowledge of the locals to locate the object of the tyrants search. The Talmud does not hold such a person liable for loss since he was instructed to show the king's agents to the property in question. He does not locate the items and bring it of his own volition. However, if he was instructed to bring barrels of wine – and left to his own discretion as to where he obtained the goods, in such a case, the Sages would hold him liable for the loss he has caused to the owner. This case illuminates the nature of the informant. If he is forced or appointed to fulfil this function, he cannot be held accountable since the state is already aware of the asset they wish to acquire. He is only an agent to achieving their means. They are not yet aware of the location of the goods, but even without him, it is within their means to eventually locate it. This is not to say that he does not assist in the search.

The auditor is only an agent for the state. He does not in actual fact have the power to harm another person; the state already controls sufficient resources to do the job without him. Since he now happens to be the one handing others to the authorities, he causes no additional harm and cannot be held accountable.

However, even though he cannot be held accountable for his actions as an auditor, perhaps his only contravention is taking the position in the first place and allowing himself to be put in such a position?

Rabbi Feinstein answers that even through choosing such a career, he does not in fact choose to implicate others. The chances are that his day to day activities will not bring him to cause undue harm in any way. He will in fact spend much of his time auditing statements which are acceptable and in most regards he will not find behaviour which is excessively fraudulent. Most cases will not require him to initiate criminal proceedings. His behaviour in all these regards will be considered to be not of his own volition since he will be required at all times to speak and act truthfully.

The Limits of *Dinah Demalchusah*

We have covered the concerns in judging someone according to secular courts and our obligations in using Jewish courts as much as possible. What then are the obligations in keeping *Dinah Demalchusa*? If the laws of the country apply, why do we seek to avoid undue harm by placing people in the criminal justice system? This appears to be a fundamental contradiction. Do we subscribe to the laws of the state and their sanction or do we avoid the system as much as possible?

The **Talmud** [7] states that *Dinah Demalchusah Dinah* – the laws of the state are laws i.e. they are applicable to us a Jews and carry the same weight as laws of the Torah. The Talmud explains as follows. If the government cuts down trees in a local valley - which belongs to private owners - and builds bridges with these trees, what right do we have to use these bridges which are built from goods expropriated and stolen from the surrounding inhabitants. We should not be gaining utility and benefit from the proceeds of theft. The principle of *Dinah Demalchusah Dinah* however, establishes that the right to expropriate is a function of the monarchy or government and the use of these bridges does not constitute a benefit from stolen resources. The government may make use of the resources of the inhabitants in the manner it sees fit. If the government takes all the trees from one individual however, it may be unnecessary for that one individual to carry all the cost. He may have a legitimate claim against the owners of all the other forests to pay him their share of the cost.

The **Rashbam**[8] explains this concept further. All taxes and excise claimed by the government are in fact legitimate. They are authorised to claim resources from the populace in order to cover the expenses of running a country. This is an inalienable right of authority. By the fact that people dwell in a particular country, they are in fact accepting upon themselves the rules and laws of that particular country. The act of electing or living in a country places us under that jurisdiction. We cannot claim that we have no intention of accepting the requirements when the act of living there already obligates us.

The **Beis Yosef** [9] quotes the opinion of the **Rashba** who explains the caveat. The concept of *Dinah Demalchusah* does not apply where it requires one to nullify requirements of the Torah. The concept will apply primarily to taxes of the state and other rules and customs of the state but not to the conduct between people. In this respect, we should use Torah guidelines to direct our conduct. If business partners are in dispute over the terms and conditions of their partnership contract, their conduct and resolution should not be resolved in secular courts. Since the Torah code should mediate the conduct between Jews, we have even less basis for referring the dispute to a secular magistrate. If however the partners are in conflict with regards to their tax compliance, for example: one wishes to avoid declaring his customs excise by importing his goods under another trade category and the other partner wishes to conduct himself with full disclosure, then the relevant state law should be used to guide their conduct.

The **Rashba** illustrates the extent of the interrelationship. If a Jew purchases land from a gentile, the Torah states that by paying the value of the land to the gentile, the gentile cedes ownership of the land. However, the *Dinah Demalchusah* may require that in order to take ownership, one may need to obtain a title deed. Someone who has no title deed has no stake or right to the land. If the buyer fails to obtain such a title deed, he has successfully seen to it that the seller cedes ownership according to Torah law, but he has not taken ownership – since *Dinah Demalchusah Dinah* demands he obtain a deed. The land is therefore ownerless until such a point as he obtains the necessary documentation. In this sense, *Dinah Demalchusah* becomes a law in actuality and is not a quasi-*Halacha*. It will have a real effect on his ownership according to *Halacha*.

The commentators are unanimous that *Dinah Demalchusah* applies to payment of taxes. They are however, divided about whether this rule applies purely in areas on financial transactions or also in all civil law. An example would be regular rules of the road. There are already very compelling halachic (Torah legal code) reasons to ensure that road rules are obeyed. The question would be whether we are also required to keep them on the basis of *Dinah Demalchusah*.

Questions for Review

1. Accountants, auditors and financial advisors are all required to report financial irregularities which may implicate their clients in fraudulent activity. Are they permitted to report these findings to the state even though their clients may punished beyond that required by the Torah?

2. May a lay-person who hears whisperings of financial irregularities approach the authorities? What are his obligations?

3. Why do Jews avoid secular courts when possible?

4. Would approaching the CCMA for labour arbitration constitute a secular court?

Sources

[1] Hilchos chova 8:9
[2] Chosen Mishpat Orach Chaim 9:11
[3] Moed Koton 17a
[4] Bava Metzia 83b
[5] Choshen Mishpat 92
[6] Bava Kamma 117
[7] Bava Basra55; Bava Kamma 113
[8] Bava Basra 55
[9] Tur Choshen Mishpat 26

PIRCHEI SHOSHANIM SHULCHAN ARUCH PROJECT

Business Ethics

Customer Value

Lesson Six

62 African Street, The Gardens, Johannesburg, South Africa tel. 076 187 1451

Table of Contents:

Customer Value

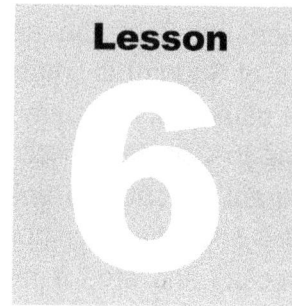

Lesson
6

Introduction and Lesson objective

Customer value is traditionally calculated as the value received by the end-consumer of a product or service. We can break down the construct of 'value' by identifying the variable components namely: utility, quality, benefits and customer satisfaction. Customer value is hard to operationalise. The variables which make up 'value' are difficult to quantify. We could measure customer satisfaction which may give a broad idea of the value associated with the product or service. We can also measure the relative cost of the product or service against a competitor. The apparent benefit to cost ratio will display some relative market-related 'value'.

As an ethical construct, customer value can take on a whole host of new variables. Customer value can reflect personality, character and integrity oriented traits which may contribute to the finished product or service. We can add value to our final offering by committing to greater levels of product safety, consumer education, after-sales service, efficient and competitive pricing, customer-based practices, ingenuous advertising and client-oriented selling techniques. Most of these principles may also be good business policies and all certainly add value to the final customer offering. This session is not about corporate philanthropy or charitable giving. It revolves around some core principles in ethical business dealings. We will expand the concept of customer-value somewhat to include even the basic obligations the business owner has towards his clients.

A Definition of Value

The following scenario quoted by **Rabbi Yehuda Itach** [1] illustrates an extreme example of conflict in values. He describes a case in the United States where a man experienced extreme food poisoning after eating in a local restaurant. His bout was so severe that he was hospitalised for several weeks at a huge personal cost to himself. He sued the restaurant and was successfully awarded $50 000. The restaurant however appealed the ruling in the appellate division and claimed that since the man, prior to his food poisoning was very overweight, the food poisoning actually helped save him thousands of dollars in weight loss regiments and potential health complications. The appeals court rescinded the original award on the strength of their argument. This anecdote is a powerful reminder of the difference between legal systems and ethical systems. The Sages teach use that the definition of *Middos Sdom* (the character traits of the inhabitants of Sodom) is where a person injures another and draws blood. Instead of paying the damages, the guilty party claims that he has really saved the wounded party from having to visit the lancer to have his blood drawn (a common healing technique). The restaurant executed a brilliant legal argument, one which saved them significant loss. *Middos Sdom* has a compelling logic. It also breaks down the ties and morals which guide a society and stop it from descending into chaos. Customer Value may be an excellent marketing instrument and is a basic for successful business. It can also be the barometer by which the value of our business transactions can be evaluated. Does the net result of our actions result in the creation of value, or purely the creation of income?

Competition and Customer Value

Mr. Rabinowitz wishes to establish a new electronics store next to the existing consumer electronics store in his local shopping district. He contends that the existing establishment does not provide for the needs of the local consumers and he wishes to provide an outlet which is better priced, offers a greater selection of premium goods and offers better pre-sales technical advice. Mr. Fischel the owner of the existing store seeks to stop his store from opening by approaching the *Beis Din*. He believes the new store is an encroachment on his rights and livelihood. Most consumers in the street are pretty excited about the new store because they believe it will give them a better choice of products and more competitive prices.

The free-market system thrives on economic competition. Competition is an enshrined western principle – the cornerstone of an open economy. Consumers ultimately suffer when industry is centralised or monopolised. It leads to economic inefficiencies, poor service and slow product development. Good customer value depends greatly on economic competition. Often, only the threat of losing market share motivates a business to ensure that customers receive identifiable value with their transactions. It is for this reason that we will explore the limitation the Jewish paradigm places on competition. As with some ethical questions, we are sometimes forced to choose between the beneficiaries. What benefits the consumer does not always benefit the vendor and certainly the opposite can be true. The Torah therefore provides a guideline to competition. The halachic considerations take the necessity for competition into account as we will explore. This is therefore the art of creating value and free enterprise without damaging the competitive vendor at the same time.

The **Talmud** [2] asks what the law should be regarding one who sets up a competing mill in the same location as an existing mill. Rav Huna the son of Rav states that there is no restriction to opening a competing mill provided the new competitor is from the same area. The new business owner will claim "whoever comes to me will come to me and whoever goes to you, will go to you." This is based on the logic that anyone should have the ability to make a livelihood in their own neighbourhood.

The **Chasam Sofer** [3] interprets this view on unrestrained competitive behaviour. He understands that competition will be permissible provided that the only loss which the existing business experiences is a loss of profit. If his livelihood will be destroyed, the Chasam Sofer forbids the competitive venture. The argument "whoever comes to me will come to me and whoever goes to you, will go to you," loses validity if the opening of the store ensures that no-one frequents the existing store at all. The Chasam Sofer states that even if the existing vendor is a wealthy man and will be able to support himself despite the closure of his business, such an activity will still be prohibited. One example of such a scenario may involve opening a shop-front at the entrance to a small courtyard in which the existing business is located. Passing traffic will likely forego entering the courtyard altogether if the required merchandise is much more accessible. **Rabbi Moshe Feinstein** broadens the implications of the Chasam Sofer's condition. He rules that destruction of livelihood, in this case, even entails destroying his ability to maintain his socioeconomic buying patterns.

Let us consider another scenario. A local organisation decides that all the local Torah bookstores charge too much for their merchandise. They have decided to open a Jewish bookstore across the road from the primary existing outlet and run their shop at break-even point. They are even offering some books at below cost as a loss-leader to get even more customers in the store. Their customers are thrilled at the prices and sales of religious books climb in the city.

Rabbi Feinstein pays particular attention to a scenario when the new venture is a not for profit. A lack of interest in making a profit becomes questionable when placed in contrast with the financial ruin of the existing establishment. The argument of the Talmud that anybody should have a right to earn a livelihood in their own town becomes moot if the purpose of the enterprise is not to make money. This argument is easier to understand if a charitable thrift shop opens up next to a legitimate profit making thrift shop. But surely in the case above, the purpose of Torah learning supersedes the injunction against competition. The Sages teach us 'kinas sofrim tarbeh chochma' - competition among scholars increases wisdom. If competition among Torah scholars is permissible, surely a Torah bookstore should also be permitted to compete. **Rabbi Ezra Basri** [4] rules that 'kinas sofrim tarbeh chochmah' does not apply to religious services – only to the scholars themselves. This seems to imply that the bookstore would not be permitted on the same grounds.

The rules of competition are many and varied and the arguments above only explore a single line of popular reasoning. In practice however, there are many different viewpoints and conclusions and a case in *Beis Din* may use alternative arguments depending on the variables of the case brought before them.

There are however a number of interesting exceptions in this discussion, with clear relevance to customer value. The **Aruch Hashulchan** [5] understands that improved pricing is a factor in allowing close competition. If the newcomer stocks different or superior brands of the same items or prices competitively but not unduly aggressively, we should permit such an enterprise. The **Chasam Sof**er [6] also believes that certain industries should be protected from competition altogether. If a critical public service cannot function properly if it is distributed among multiple providers, we should endeavour to disallow competition. In this case, competition will result in reduced utility to the consumer, not improved. We can imagine a scenario of the importer of religious products in a small town. He is only able to afford the costs of shipping because he is able to order stock in the appropriate quantities. It is unreasonable that we should allow others to enter this industry on the basis that it will result in neither business surviving.

Gneivas Daas – Honesty in Advertising

Mr. Sacks runs a clothing store and decided to run a promotion to pick up his flagging business during the recession. Ordinarily he orders cheap clothing from China in addition to his higher quality fare manufactured locally. He advertises Chinese-made suits as "Imported European Styles" and sells them at a much greater margin than he usually makes. He has justified his actions on the basis that the advert is entirely true. The suits are in fact imported and they are styled according to European trends.

The **Talmud** [7] discusses the injunction against *gneivas daas* (lit: stealing the mind of another). It is forbidden to steal the mind of anyone - Jew and non-Jew alike. This includes offering gifts that the giver knows the receiver will not accept. This creates goodwill based on an action that the giver has no intention of following through. The Talmud does state however, that if the intention is to show honour to the person involved, even though they are unlikely to accept the gesture, then it should be permitted. *Gneivas daas* is any action which serves to mislead others concerning your intentions or actions.

One practical application of this rule is minor defects in merchandise. A salesman is required to disclose any defect or detraction in the merchandise he is selling if he believes that the presence of such a defect may influence the decision of the buyer [8]. While this may seem simple, there are scenarios where a salesman might feel more justified in glossing over limitations of the product. If a software salesman believes that his client probably requires a feature which his software lacks, he may feel it unnecessary to disclose that fact since the client didn't ask for it specifically.

Mr. Sacks may have told the truth in the advert, but it was specifically designed to deceive. We see that misleading others in this case is not a function of the action, rather the purpose of the deceiver.

Let us look at another scenario. Mr. Cohen is a medical aid and short term insurance broker and advertises his services as an insurance and financial advisor. He is an agent for a single basket of insurance options from a single company because he likes their services, the products he offers are simple to understand and they pay higher commissions than other financial service providers. Is he permitted to advertise his services as an advisor if his primary function is to promote a limited repertoire of financial goods?

The **Shulchan Aruch** [9] states that we cannot take advantage of others' misperceptions about our intentions. In South Africa, where financial advisors often represent a single company, most consumers are aware that they are promoting a particular range of products and the terminology might be appropriate. We should however be cognisant of the possibility of misdirection.

Mekach Taos – What Did I Just Buy?

The **Shulchan Aruch** [10] states that whenever a person purchases an item, he intends to buy an item without defects – unless he specifically states otherwise. The concept of a mistaken purchase – *mekach taos* – has its roots in *gneivas daas* or misleading another. The application however is with regard to a transaction whose true nature has been deliberately or mistakenly hidden and the subsequent voiding of the sale. As we will see, *mekach taos* can function both ways. It is also possible that a trader will sell an item whose true value he was unaware of at a price well below its actual worth. In the case of a defect, we need to measure that defect against the standard in the marketplace. If a vendor sells an apple with a minor blemish which only becomes apparent when the purchaser returns home, we need to assess if the blemish is something which most people would accept as a normal occurrence. If however, the fruit is spoiled and sold in such a way that the purchaser would not notice, the object is a *mekach taos* and the original sale is void.

Mr. Levy finds an old violin in his attic and takes it to be evaluated on the Antiques Road Show. The evaluator makes a mistake in the evaluation and decides that the violin has sentimental value only. Mr. Levy sells it to Goldwasser Musical Emporium for a nominal fee. A week later his grandmother informs him that the violin is in fact a limited edition instrument with significant antiquity and musical value. Mr. Levy would like to know if he can reverse the sale.

The **Shulchan Aruch** [11] will allow him to void the sale. Since Mr. Levy sold an item when its true value was not disclosed, neither party was engaged in a legitimate purchase. There is no basis for allowing the sale to go through. In this case the *mekach taos* will also protect the rights of the seller. The intention of the seller and subsequent acceptance by the purchaser need to be established. This becomes a concern when goods are sold 'as is'. Chances are, the seller is aware of the limitations of the product and does not want the purchaser to demand recourse.

There are however, exceptions. If Mr. Levy found an ancient book in a *hefker* (ownerless) pile at an old shul and sold the book to the local dealer, provided they both understand the nature of the item, the sale goes through. The dealer however, locates a valuable manuscript tucked into the cover of the book. Is he required to pay the seller the additional value? In this case, the **Mordechai** [12] explains that the sale is complete. Since the original owner never really 'acquired' the manuscript – he was never aware it was there – the new owner takes ownership and is not required to buy it. When the value of the item was unknown, the sale is void since there is no clear understanding of the value; the ownership of the item however is clear. In the event of a 'hidden' item, the value of the ostensible purchase was known by both parties. The ownership of the hidden item comes into question. Since ownership requires a level of awareness, the hidden item is claimed by the first to notice it.

The underlying principle is clear. Business transactions with customers require transparency in order to even be considered real purchases. While added value is a critical element in effective business, basic value also needs to be the starting point. Once we compete ethically and honestly, we can continue to add value to our initial offerings.

Questions for Review

1. Should we limit the number of Kosher restaurants on the basis of unfair competition or should the free-market system run unchecked resulting in only the best establishments surviving?

2. Are we more concerned with the concept of adding consumer value to the lives of many people or does the economic welfare of several individuals take precedence?

3. Are documents, contracts and fine print which use excessive jargon considered *gneivas daas*, if they are unlikely to be fully understood by the person signing it?

4. A lawyer guarantees a potential client that if the plaintiff uses his services, he is guaranteed to win his case. After losing the case, is the original agreement that the lawyer and client entered into a *mekach taos*? Does it make a difference if the lawyer intended to deceive or not?

Sources

[1] *Sefer Nesivos Sochir*
[2] *Bava Basra 21b*
[3] *Choshen Mishpat 61*
[4] *Shaarei Ezra 2:131*
[5 *Choshen Mishpat 156:11*
[6] *Choshen Mishpat 79*
[7] *Chullin 94a*

[8] Sma Choshen Mishpat 228:7
[9] Choshen Mishpat 228
[10] Choshen Mishpat 232:6
[11] Choshen Mishpat 227:14
[12] Choshen Mishpat 248

Business Ethics

Insolvency, Company Status and Limited Liabilities

Lesson Seven

Table of Contents:

Insolvency, Company Status and Limited Liabilities

- with a look at the New Companies Act

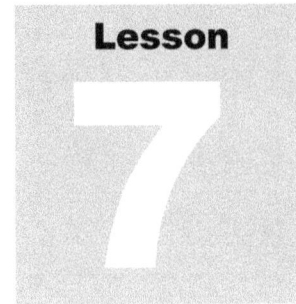

Lesson 7

Introduction and Lesson Objective

The New Companies Act 2008 which was gazetted in April 2009, effectively overhauls the previous Companies Act of 1973 in its entirety. Along with this transition, 30 years of accumulated case law and legal principle have been overpowered and accepted business practices need to be carefully reviewed. While the Companies Act of 1973 makes provision for and holds directors accountable for reckless trading, the New Companies Act reduces the burden of proving reckless and fraudulent behaviour. The Act holds directors unswervingly responsible for their actions if it is found that they directed their business to act in an unlawful or fraudulent manner. What warrants even greater attention is that directors can now also be held directly responsible for trading in a state of insolvency. While traditionally commercial insolvency, in which the business is unable to continue its operations and service its liabilities, would be a natural interpretation; the Act does not clarify the term. Factual insolvency, in which the liabilities exceed the assets of the business, could be another scenario. This situation may however arise due to shareholders loans which are not enforceable. This would have the effect of maintaining the liquidity of the business even while the liabilities of the business exceed the assets. While the intention of the Act is most likely not to punish executive who run their businesses profitably; there will need to be more vigilance by company executive as to the solvency status of their business.

While the New Companies Act will carry greater implication for directors and officers, the Jewish ethical code also requires greater ethical standards of corporations and their custodians. We will discuss the limitations of a limited liability company as well as the concept of bankruptcy and whether it absolves the owners of the company from the underlying debts.

The Status of a Limited Liability Company

Mr. Friedman is concerned about the implications of his newest investment. He has purchased a stake in a PTY Ltd which he and his new partners are trying to rescue and turn into a profitable business. At present, the business has assets only slightly exceeding their liabilities. He is concerned however, that one of the payables, Mr. Stein will claim against him before the company has an opportunity to settle the debt. Can Mr.

Stein claim his debt directly from Mr. Friedman as he is the only Jewish shareholder of this business?

Central to the idea of corporations is their status in Jewish law. Do we accord the corporation the status of an individual – a single entity or is it in fact a partnership – one with innumerable partners. This is by no means a fastidious definition. By understanding the nature of the corporation, we establish the proper means of dispute resolution, responsibility for debt and the status of the company directors.

The majority of contemporary experts define the corporation as a partnership. An ordinary partnership which is not incorporated with one or two partners can, in the event the partners are Jewish, be taken to *Beis Din*. The **Minchas Yitzchok** [1] rules that even in the case of a company or corporation which ordinarily protects it's shareholder from liability – if the shareholders are Jewish, and provided that we can 'lift the corporate veil' and see that they were acting in their own self-interest – one may claim against the shareholders themselves. This idea certainly has precedent in commercial law as well. A company cannot be used as a vehicle for avoiding liability when the responsibility for the debt is attributable to the shareholders themselves.

The **Shulchan Aruch** [2] states that a single partner can be held accountable according to their percentage holding. This would affect a business which is composed of Jews and non-Jews alike. The claimant could take the Jewish partner to *Beis Din* to hold him accountable according to his percentage of the shares. This would obviously not be possible in the case of a public company.

Bankruptcy – Is There a Way Out?

Mr. Silver's business is commercially insolvent and is no longer able to trade. He declares bankruptcy and his payables receive a small settlement from the auctioning of his assets. He still has significant personal assets overseas as well as trust funds of which his wife and children are the official beneficiaries. Mr. Kaplan who has just been paid out 10% of what he is owed is now also facing foreclosure. Is he entitled to still make a claim against Mr. Silver?

How does the Torah treat bankruptcy? The **Minchas Chinuch** [3] states that it is a Torah obligation to pay one's debts. This obligation however does not take bankruptcy into account. There are various provisions for one who cannot pay his debts including the sale and attachment of his assets. What is clearly evident however, is that there is no allowance made for bankruptcy. The debt remains valid until such a time as he is able to pay. We are however required to maintain the laws of the country we live in. Is it not sufficient that legal systems around the world make allowance for bankruptcy? It is discussable whether the concept of *dinah demalchusa* (the laws of the land) applies to obligations between one person and another. In one place, it seems from the **Shulchan**

Aruch [4] that interpersonal dealings are not bound by the limitations of Dinah D'Malchusa. (Please see appendix A for further clarification). The **Shach** [5] notes an important prerequisite that these laws of the state do not contradict Torah law. If the state requires that Jews cease performing *bris milah,* we are by no means required to follow their ruling. The most common application of this law is taxation. In this scenario, even if the state has ruled that Mr. Silver has performed all his obligations towards those who are owed money, our own code demands that he still honours his debts. The debt he owes Mr. Kaplan is not between him and the state, even though the state has ruled on it. Furthermore, since his debt is a matter of *halachic* obligation, the state ruling will not exonerate his Torah obligation.

There is another concept which may permit the concept of bankruptcy. The **Shulchan Aruch**[6] states that common business agreement procedures are applicable in practice. **Rabbi Yaakov Blau** [7] understands that all company loans and issued credit will be subject to common business processes. He quotes the **Rashba** who takes the concept of the Shulchan Aruch one step further. He states that the concept of 'common business procedure' applies to all business processes, not just agreements. Says Rabbi Blau, by initiating in a business relationship with another person or business which incorporates loans and credit, a trader essentially agrees that their relationship should be governed by prevailing business custom – to the inclusion of the concept of bankruptcy. How does he show his agreement to the terms of business? Since the corporation is by nature a 'non-real' entity, by trading though such a mechanism we indicate our acceptance of the concept and are therefore bound by the rules managing such an entity. Private loans will not be included in this category. Since at the time of the loan, no one has any intention of applying standard business rules to a private loan, the lender should always be able to make a claim for the full value of his loan. There are additional experts who concur with this ruling and the general trend today is that bankruptcy laws do apply in general course of business. While this is the trend, there may be exceptions based on the principles outlined above.

What About the CEO?

Mr. Jacobson is the CEO of All African Investments PTY (Ltd). During his short tenure, he is the pioneer for some disastrous and reckless decisions which halve the value of the company's managed retirement funds. He is currently under investigation for his obvious role in these events. Mr. Shneider, whose provident fund was badly scorched, has approached *Beis Din* as a means to holding Mr. Jacobson liable for his losses.

What ultimately is the status of an appointed director or manager of a corporation? This is relevant to the amount of responsibility he must carry for his decisions. In Jewish law, there are two models which may justifiably apply to the CEO of a business. Is the CEO a *shaliach* (legal representative) or an *apotropos* (custodian or trustee)?

A *shaliach* does not act of his own volition. He acts in accordance with a clear set of instructions. A *shaliach* does not make any decisions; he stands in the place of his primary and performs an action that the primary is unable or does not wish to conclude. He is treated in *Halacha* (Jewish law) as if the action was performed by the primary himself. This is different from a CEO who acts in accordance with a mandate but ultimately is responsible for his own actions. The *apotropos* is the custodian of assets for orphans, the disabled or someone who is absent. He acts in much the same way as a trustee – he is mandated to look after the assets or business – he is not however a shareholder. His actions however in this capacity are virtually unlimited provided his overarching goal is the care of the assets. He must very carefully focus on using the money for the benefit of the beneficiaries. He may not use the money in a way which exposes it to unnecessary risk or for the purposes of charity.

All debts incurred by the business during the tenure of any CEO must be paid from the funds of the business. The **Shulchan Aruch** [8] introduces us to the idea of transactions which have no basis in Jewish law but yet still carry the implications of all other debts. This transaction (*kinyan situmpta*) means that even though corporate debt does not have the same bearing *halachically* as a personal loan, debtors will still be able to claim their money from other assets of the business. The traditional alternative debt collection process in the Talmud allows one to attach the property of the *ba'al chov* – the party who owes the money. This would effectively allow one to claim corporate property in lieu of a debt.

Can we then, claim directly from the CEO who mismanaged the company in the first place? Based on our understanding of the role of both the CEO and the corporations, it seems unlikely that such an act will be possible. The CEO is a custodian and may carry responsibility for the funds in his care. As such, the corporation could legitimately claim money from him which he lost through gross negligence. The client, in this case Mr. Schneider, will be unable to claim directly from the CEO but should be entitled to claim from the corporation. According to *Halacha*, if the company is unable to honour his claim, he should be permitted to claim from the property of the business. If, as in our case, the company is incorporated into South African law, and both the claims against the CEO for remuneration and Mr. Schneider's claim against the company will be coordinated by the state; Mr. Schneider will likely have no real recourse outside traditional courts since *Beis Din* will be unable to contend with the company in this case.

Questions for Review

1. If a party to a business transaction states proactively that he does not wish to be subject to traditional business transactions such as bankruptcy, can he remove its applicability altogether ?

2. Is the ruling of Rabbi Blau with regard to Bankruptcy likely to encourage lending and commerce or place it under greater suspicion?

3. Why could *Dinah Demalchusa* not apply in the case of money debts owed?

4. What implications should be enforced on an Officer who is found to have managed his company negligently? Is it appropriate according to *Halacha* to claim the loss against his own personal assets?

5. What role could *Beis Din* play in assisting the victim of corporate mismanagement? Is there any form of recourse available?

Sources

[1] *Chelek 3:1*
[2] *Choshen Mishpat 176*
[3] *Minchas Chinuch 259*
[4] *Choshen Mishpat 68:1*
[5] *Choshen Mishpat 73:36*
[6] *Choshen Mishpat 201*
[7] *Pischei Choshen Halvo'o 12*
[8] *Choshen Mishpat 201*

Appendix A

Dinah D'Malchusa

Dinah D'Malchusa translates as the law of the land. The Sage Shmuel, one of the leaders of the Babylonian Exile stated many times that "The law of the land is the law"[1]. There is however, a discussion amongst the Rishonim[2] as to whether this law applies between citizens (horizontally) or whether this law applies only to laws relating directly between Government and citizens (vertically).

The Sefer HaTerumos (46:5) [3] explains that the Tsarphatim[4] hold that Shmuel only said that "The law of the country is the law" regarding things that directly affect the Government's revenue: that is taxes and toll charges. However, if the government made a law, such as forcing a lender to accept a smaller return on a loan due to hard times, Torah Law would require that the full amount be returned. Whereas the opinion of the Ramban[5] is that "the law of the land is the law" also applies horizontally. The Ramban proves this from a gemora[6]. The gemora learns out regarding a "gift document", a court document stating that a present was given, is valid due to the principle of Dinah D'Malchusa Dinah – "The law of the land is the law". Just as the law of the land applies to gift documents so too it applies to other laws between citizens.

There is much debate as to which way the final halacha comes out, whether like the Tsarfatim or the Ramban. It is worthy to note that the Shach[7]concludes like the Ramban, in that he paskens (decides the law) that "The law of the land is the law" in many cases relating to laws between citizens.

---

[1] Baba Basra 55a
[2] A School of French (and German) Tulmudic analysts who lived in the 12th and 13th centaury
[3] Rabbi Yitchak Shmelkes late 19th Centaury
[4] Baalei Tosfos around 1200-1400
[5] Rabbi Moshe Ben Nachaman d.1270
[6] Baba Basra 55a
[7] Rabbi Shabsai HaKohen of Vilna (1622-1663) in his glosses on Yoreh Deah 165:8